KT-116-652

Contents

Introduction

Beads and beadwork have captivated people for thousands of years. Ever since men and women were able to collect shells and seeds and string them on to animal <u>sinew</u> or thin strips of leather, they have been making and wearing beadwork. Beads have played an important part in many cultures across the world, the most famous of these being the <u>Zulu</u> tribes in South Africa and the <u>Native Americans</u>.

Both loose beads and finished beadwork have been used as currency and items to trade over the generations.

Beads can be made from a wide range of materials: there are bone beads from India; Venetian glass beads from Italy; Bohemian glass beads from the Czech Republic; shell, horn and bone beads from the Philippines; ceramic beads from Greece and Peru; seed beads and bugle beads from Japan; plastic beads from the Far East; as well as precious metal beads; semi-precious beads such as amethyst, rose quartz and amber; and beads made from seeds and berries.

Beads can be strung to make a simple yet elegant necklace or bracelet, like our Ethnic Pendant. The smaller seed beads can be stitched and woven together to make more intricate patterns and designs as with our Mini Bag and Friendship Bracelet. Beads are also used to decorate other objects such as our Trinket Pot.

We now have such a wide range of beads to choose from it is often hard to know where to start! The beads featured in these projects are mainly high quality Japanese seed beads and Bohemian glass beads from

FUNKY FACT!

The colours and patterns of beads hold special significance for the Zulu people of South Africa. Teenaged girls make 'love letters' by weaving beads in to jewellery. The colours and patterns contain hidden messages for their sweetheart. The girls give their 'love letters' to boys, who keep them as treasured possessions.

Start to
Bead

Jill Thomas

SEARCH PRESS

First published in paperback in Great Britain 2008
Search Press Ltd
Wellwood
North Farm Road
Tunbridge Wells
Kent TN2 3DR

Published in hardback by Search Press 2007

ISBN: 978-1-84448-391-4

The Publishers and authors can accept no responsibility for any consequences arising from the information, advice or instructions given in this publication.

Suppliers
If you have difficulty obtaining any of the materials and equipment mentioned in this book, please visit the author's website:
www.gjbeads.co.uk
or the Search Press website:
www.searchpress.com

Some words are underlined <u>like this</u>. They are explained in the glossary on page 48.

For Jenny and Jeff, with special thanks to my mum and dad for all their support and encouragement.

The publishers would like to thank consultant Rebecca Vickers and also the following for appearing in the photographs:
Lucia Brisefer, Katherine Chandrain, Charlie de la Bédoyère, Nicole Fields, Ben Kersey and Katrina Hindley.

Printed in China

the Czech Republic which are widely available and reasonably priced, which in turn will give a professional finish to your beadwork.

Beading is a wonderful hobby and is even more fun to share with your friends. Wear your own jewellery and listen to the compliments from your friends and family. Even better, make a necklace and give it as a birthday gift, people will be thrilled and amazed that you made it! Why not have a bead party: invite some friends over one evening and share your new jewellery making skills with them.

Materials

❋ Beads

● • • • • • • • • • **Seed beads** These are small glass beads with a central hole, usually 2mm or less in diameter. Japanese size 11 seed beads are the most widely used seed beads in <u>beadweaving</u>, and they are usually available in the largest colour range. They are called size 11 because of the old sizing system. There were approximately 11 beads per inch (2.5cm). Likewise, size 8 seed beads are 8 per inch. There are several ways of writing size 11, such as SZ11, 11/0 or 11° but they all refer to the same size bead. Seed beads are sometimes called rocailles.

● • • • • • • • • • **Bugle beads** These are long, tube-shaped beads. Japanese bugle beads are available from 2mm (1/16in) up to 30mm (1¼in), although the most common sizes available are 3mm (1/8in), 6mm (¼in) and 9mm (3/8in). Sometimes the ends of the bugles can be sharp or cracked. Do not use these in your beadwork as they may cut the thread.

● • • • • • • • • • **Magatama drops** High quality Japanese magatama beads have a large hole in comparison to the size of the bead, they are great for adding texture and depth to your beadwork designs.

● • • • • • • • • • **Cube beads** The most common size is 4mm (1/8in). Cube beads have a relatively large hole for the size of bead.

● • • • • • • • • • **Metal beads** These are small spacer beads, usually gold or silver coloured. They are ideal to add some sparkle to the other beads in your design. We used them in the Charm Bracelet pattern.

● • • • • • • • • • **Ceramic beads** These often have a matt finish, which contrasts wonderfully with the shiny finish of glass beads.

● • • • • • • • • • **Bohemian glass beads** These are from the Czech Republic. There is a huge range, including round, <u>faceted</u> or <u>fire-polished</u> beads, as well as different shapes such as the hearts, stars and flowers used in the Charm Bracelet on page 22.

❋ Storage containers

There is a wide variety of storage containers on the market. These little triangular dishes are great to sort your beads while you are working, but you will find storage boxes with individual compartments and well fitting lids ideal for storing your beads while not in use.

size 11 seed beads

4mm (1/8in) cube beads

size 6 seed beads

magatama drops

size 8 seed beads

6mm (¼in) bugles

✸ Shell pendants

These are fashioned from real shells from the Philippines. They are available in dozens of designs and colours and truly become the centrepiece of your necklace.

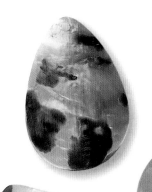

Shell pendants for making beaded jewellery.

✸ Needles and threads

Beading needles These are usually about 50mm (2in) long, although different lengths are available. They have a very small eye, which makes threading the needle a bit of a challenge sometimes, but the eye needs to be small to allow the needle to pass through the tiny seed beads.

Nymo This is a nylon beading thread, and beads hang nicely from it because it is not twisted. It is available in several thicknesses: B is medium, which is ideal for most projects and D is a little thicker and is used with larger beads or when firmer tension is required.

Nymo, clear elastic cord and jewellery cable, all used in beading projects.

Clear elastic cord This is available in 0.5mm, 0.7mm and 1mm thicknesses. The elastic does not fray like other elastic and the clear colour makes it ideal to use with any colour of beads.

Jewellery cable Soft, flexible wire specially for making jewellery. It is available in several thicknesses and is nice and strong. It is ideal when you want to string beads on to a straight wire, as in the Ethnic Pendant and the Charm Bracelet. We have used 0.46mm (0.018in) jewellery cable in both these projects.

✵ Findings

These are the little bits and pieces used with beads and threads to make beaded jewellery.

(1) **Filigree bell caps** Thread one each side of a large glass bead to decorate it.

(2) **Split rings** Two rings of wire that look like tiny key-rings. They are ideal for using with a lobster clasp at the end of a necklace or bracelet.

(3) **Jump rings** are made from a single ring of wire. They are used to attach pendants.

(4) **Crimp tubes** Crimp tubes and crimp beads are used with jewellery cable, instead of knotting, to secure the end of a necklace. You squash the tube or bead in place using chain-nosed pliers. Crimp tubes are much softer and easier to work with than crimp beads.

(5) **Lobster clasps** One of the most common and easy to use clasps. Use it with a split ring when fastening a necklace or bracelet.

(6) **Magnetic clasps** These contain a magnet and just snap together. They are great for bracelets or for people who find clasps difficult to manage. Do not use a magnetic clasp if the person who will wear the jewellery has a heart pacemaker.

(7) **Headpins** These are long pins with a head on one end. You can use them to make charms, as in the Charm Bracelet on page 22.

✵ Safety pins

These are available in a variety of sizes for jewellery making. The most commonly available sizes are 28mm (1¹⁄₈in) and 34mm (1³⁄₈in). You can buy them in gold and silver as well as funky colours such as pink, purple, green and blue.

Acrylic paints and paint brushes are used for painting trinket pots.

Trinket pots

You can buy these little wooden pots at bead stores. They are ideal for decorating with beads. They are all the same size, which is great to work with while following a pattern. You can paint them the colour you want with acrylic paints. Choose small paint brushes to give a neat finish to the paintwork.

Tools

Old scissors Use these for cutting jewellery cable if you do not have cable snips available.

Round-nosed pliers These are used for bending and shaping wire. They are great for forming loops in the tops of headpins.

Side cutters These are ideal for cutting and trimming wire and headpins.

Chain-nosed pliers These are for squashing crimp tubes or beads on jewellery cable.

Small, sharp scissors You need these to trim and cut Nymo and clear elastic cord for beading projects.

Cable snips These pliers are specially made for cutting jewellery cable. Do not use them on wire and headpins, as they will get blunt very quickly.

Bead mats

Bead mats make the ideal working surface, they are soft and comfortable to work on and prevent your beads rolling away.

Indian bead loom

This inexpensive loom is ideal for making friendship bracelets and other small projects.

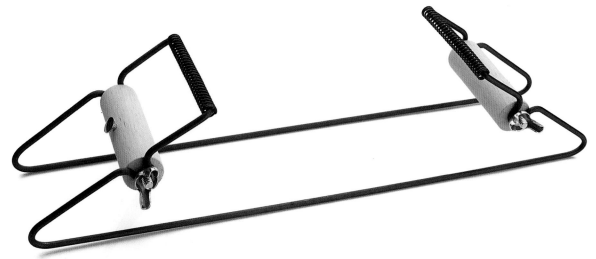

Ethnic Pendant

The brown lip shell pendant makes the perfect centrepiece for this necklace and looks beautiful with the natural colours of the beads. This is a good project to start with as stringing beads on jewellery cable is a quick and easy way to make necklaces or bracelets.

You will need

Chain-nosed pliers

One 7mm (¼in) jump ring

Shell pendant

150cm (59in) of jewellery cable

Cable snips or old scissors

Two silver crimp tubes

Silver lobster clasp

Ninety-six bronze 4mm beads

Thirty ceramic 6 x 3mm beads

One 5mm (³/₁₆in) split ring

1 Use the chain-nosed pliers to open the jump ring. Bend one side of the ring forwards to open up the gap.

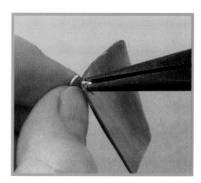

2 Place the jump ring in the hole in the shell pendant and use the chain-nosed pliers to close the ring.

3 Cut 150cm (59in) of flexible jewellery cable using cable snips or old scissors.

TOP TIP!

You do not need to use a needle with jewellery cable, as you can use the end of the cable to pick up beads.

4 Use the end of the cable to pick up a silver crimp tube.

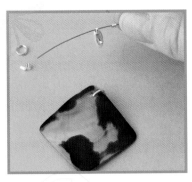

5 Pick up the lobster clasp in the same way.

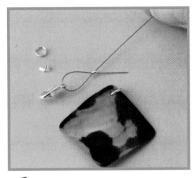

6 Bend back the end of the cable and push it back through the crimp tube.

7 Use the chain-nosed pliers to squash the crimp tube flat. This secures the clasp end of the necklace.

8 Use cable snips or old scissors to trim the tail of the jewellery cable to around 1cm (³/₈in).

9 Thread three bronze beads on to the cable, and tuck the trimmed tail into the first bead to hide it.

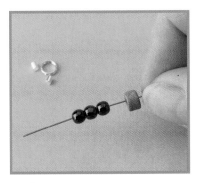

10 Thread on a ceramic bead and three more bronze beads.

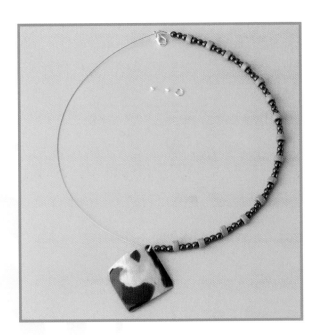

11 Repeat this pattern until you have threaded on fifteen ceramic beads and sixteen sets of bronze beads. Then thread on the pendant as shown.

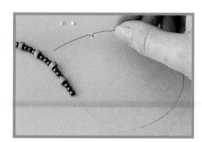

1 2 Bead the other side of the necklace in exactly the same way. Then thread on another silver crimp tube and the split ring.

1 3 Put the end of the cable back through the crimp tube and two of the bronze beads.

1 4 Pull the cable through and tighten it so that the loop going into the split ring is the same size as the one at the other end of the necklace, going into the clasp.

1 5 Squash the crimp tube using chain-nosed pliers.

Dress up any outfit with this easy to make Ethnic Pendant.

1 6 Trim the end of the cable as close as possible to the bronze bead, using cable snips or old scissors.

The finished clasp.

What next?

Experiment with other pendant shapes and different colour combinations. Use the colours in the pendant to help you choose the bead colours.

Safety Pin Bracelet

Choose coloured safety pins to make this wonderful bracelet. It is amazing how the shining beads transform the safety pins into something really elegant!

You will need

Thirty 34mm (1³/₈in) pink safety pins

120 (or 5g) size 8 pink seed beads

Sixty (or 7g) pink 4mm cubes

Thirty 6mm fire-polished beads

Chain-nosed pliers

Two 30cm (12in) lengths of 1mm clear elastic cord

Ninety (or 6g) size 6 pink seed beads

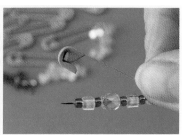

1 Open a safety pin and thread on a size 8 pink seed bead, a pink cube, another pink seed bead, a 6mm fire-polished bead, a pink seed bead, a pink cube and a pink seed bead. Note that all the pink seed beads that go on the safety pins should be size 8.

2 Close the safety pin and use chain-nosed pliers to squash the fastening end of the pin as shown. This will seal it closed. Make thirty of these beaded safety pins.

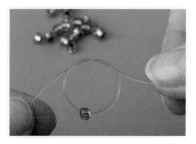

3 Take your 30cm (12in) length of clear elastic cord. Tie on a size 6 seed beads 5cm (2in) from the end.

4 Thread on three size 6 pink seed beads.

TOP TIP!

If you use safety pins or beads of a different size, you might find that you can not fit all the beads on your safety pin. If this happens, miss out one or two of the seed beads on the pin. Likewise if you have a gap, add extra beads to fill the safety pin.

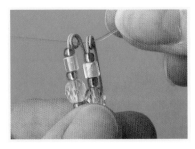

5 Thread on two beaded safety pins through the narrow ends.

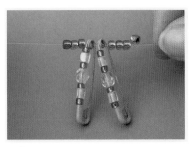

6 Add three more size 6 seed beads.

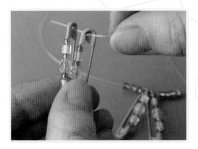

7 Add another two safety pins, threading them through the fastening end this time.

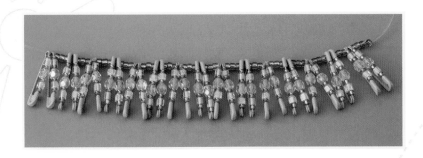

8 Repeat steps 4 to 7 until all the safety pins are threaded on to the clear elastic cord.

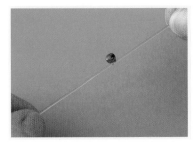

9 Take the second 30cm (12in) length of clear elastic cord and tie on a size 6 pink seed bead as before.

10 Push the elastic through the fastening part of one safety pin, at the bottom of the bracelet.

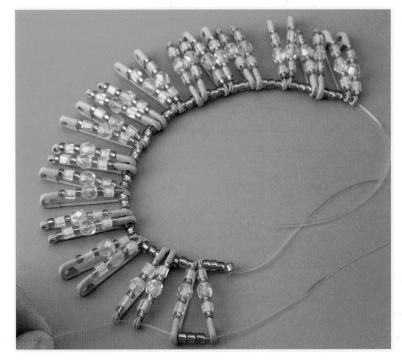

11 Thread on three size 6 pink seed beads and go through the fastening end of the next safety pin. Then go through the narrow end of the next safety pin as shown.

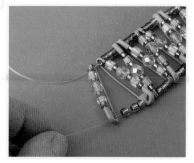

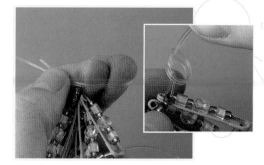

|2 Thread on three more size 6 seed beads and go through the next safety pin's narrow end. Then go through the fastening end of the next safety pin.

|3 Thread on three more size 6 seed beads and go through the fastening end of the next safety pin. Continue in this way round the bracelet.

|4 Remove the knotted size 6 seed bead that you started with at the beginning of the top of the bracelet. Bring the beginning and end of the top elastic together and tie an overhand knot as shown.

TOP TiP!

If you find that the knot slips, simply pull even tighter so that it holds.

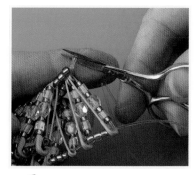

|5 Pull tight so that the knot will hold.

|6 Trim the ends close to the knot.

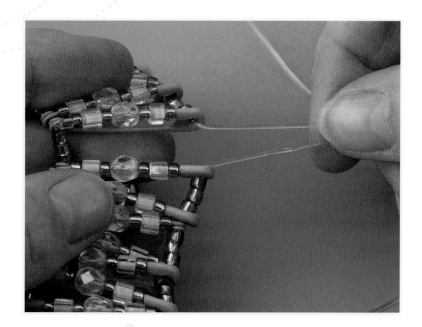

|7 Remove the knotted bead from the elastic at the bottom of the bracelet and repeat steps 14 to 16 to finish the bracelet.

What next?

Once you have learned the technique for this bracelet, try designing your own. The secret is to make sure that each safety pin is filled with beads.

Your friends will be amazed when they find out that your lovely bracelet is made from safety pins!

Daisy Ring

You will need

1m (39½in) Nymo B beading thread

Beading needle

Sixty (or more) purple size 11 seed beads

Fifteen (or more) white size 11 seed beads

This cute little daisy ring is great to make, wear and share for a bright, summery look. We have made a ring of fifteen flowers, but you will test the size on your finger and you may need to add more flowers so that the ring will fit.

These rings only use a few beads, so they are great for using up small quantities of beads left over from other projects.

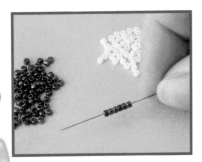

1 Thread the beading needle with 1m (39½in) of beading thread. Pick up six purple size 11 seed beads on the needle.

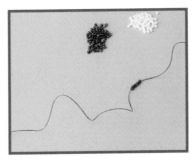

2 Slide the beads down the thread, leaving a 15cm (6in) tail.

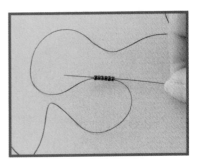

3 Bring the needle back round and stitch through the six beads again in the same direction.

4 Pull the thread through to create a little loop as shown.

5 Pull the loop to make a little circle.

6 Tie a reef knot. First tie left over right.

7 Then tie right over left. Pull the knot tight.

8 Pick up one white bead on the needle and stitch through the third bead in the circle.

9 Push the white bead into the centre of the circle with your thumb.

10 Pick up two purple seed beeds and one white.

11 Stitch down through a purple bead on the right-hand side of the daisy.

12 Pull the thread through.

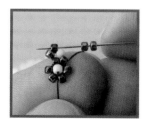

13 Pick up two purple beads and stitch through the top purple bead.

14 Pull through to complete the second daisy.

15 Repeat steps 10 to 14 to make a row of daisies.

16 Test the size of the ring on your finger. This picture shows a ring of fifteen flowers. You may need to do up to twenty.

17 Pick up a purple bead and put the needle through the first two beads of the first daisy you made.

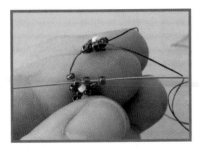

18 Pick up another purple bead and stitch through the last two beads in the daisy chain.

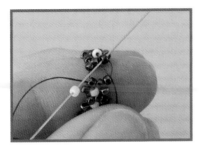

19 Pick up a white seed bead and stitch diagonally across from the end of the chain, through a bead at the beginning.

20 Stitch through five beads around the daisy you have just made.

21 Stitch under the thread between two beads.

22 Pull the thread through to make a loop and stitch through it.

23 Stitch through another five beads.

24 Trim the end of the thread. Rethread the needle with the tail of thread you left at the beginning, and repeat steps 21 to 24 to finish this thread.

The delicate Daisy Ring.

What next?

Make daisy rings for all your friends, or a whole handful for yourself! You could also keep on beading with the daisy pattern to make a bracelet or necklace. Stitch on a lobster clasp and a split ring to fasten the ends together.

Charm Bracelet

This shimmering turquoise bracelet is dripping with beautiful charms. This one has sixteen charms but you might find that you need to make the bracelet longer and add more charms. The beads we have used are listed but you could buy a pick and mix selection of assorted Czech glass beads.

1 Take a headpin and pick up a clear size 8 seed bead, a filigree bell cap, a 6mm fire-polished bead, a filigree cap and another clear size 8 seed bead.

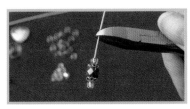

2 Use the side cutters to trim the headpin about 1cm (3/8in) from the beads.

Stay Safe!

Hold on to the end of the headpin when you trim it. It might fly off and hurt you.

3 Hold the trimmed headpin with round-nosed pliers.

4 Turn the pliers as shown to make a loop.

5 Complete the turn to close the loop.

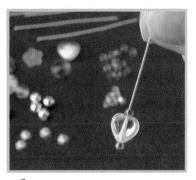

6 Take another headpin and thread on a turquoise seed bead, a 10mm heart and another turquoise seed bead. Trim the headpin and loop the end as before.

7 Make two each of all the charm drops shown here, so that you have sixteen drops for your bracelet.

8 Cut a 30cm (11¾in) length of jewellery cable using cable snips or old scissors.

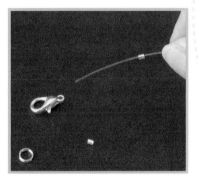

9 Thread a crimp tube on to the end of the jewellery cable.

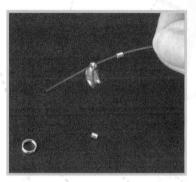

10 Thread on a lobster clasp.

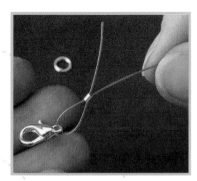

11 Thread the end of the cable back through the crimp tube to make a loop.

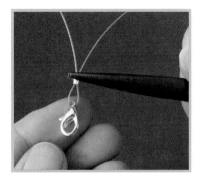

12 Use chain-nosed pliers to squash the crimp tube.

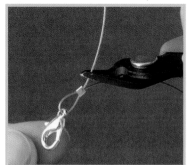

13 Trim the end of the cable to about 1cm (³⁄₈in) from the crimp tube using cable snips or old scissors.

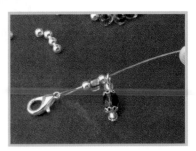

14 Thread on a 3mm silver bead, a size 5 turquoise triangle bead and another silver bead.

15 Slide the beads down to the clasp end of the cable so that they cover the trimmed end.

16 Thread on one of the charms you have made.

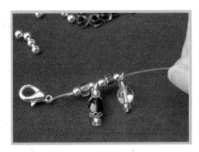

17 Thread on a silver 3mm bead, a turquoise triangle bead, a silver 3mm bead and a second charm.

18 Thread on all the charms in the same way, with silver and turquoise beads in between, then thread on a crimp tube and a split ring.

19 Feed the end of the cable back through the crimp tube and two more beads.

20 Use chain-nosed pliers to squash the crimp tube.

21 Trim the end of the cable as close as possible to the beads, using cable snips or old scissors.

Wear your finished Charm Bracelet with pride – it will charm everyone who sees it!

What next?

An anklet is just a little longer than a bracelet and will give you a fantastic, exotic look. You could complete the set with a necklace as well. How charming can you get?

Trinket Pot

You can buy these little trinket pots at bead stores and paint them any colour you want with acrylic paint. Decorate them with bead netting and you have a wonderful gift that anyone would be delighted to receive.

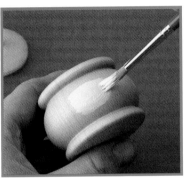

| Paint the pot and lid with the cream acrylic paint. Leave one coat to dry, then paint a second coat.

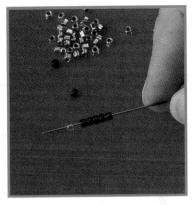

2 Thread the needle with the beading thread and pick up five plum seed beads and one gold. Push the beads down the thread, leaving a 15cm (6in) tail.

3 Repeat this fifteen times, so that you finish with fifteen gold beads on the thread.

4 Take the needle round to the end of the thread to make a circle. Push the needle through all the beads again, around ten at a time as shown.

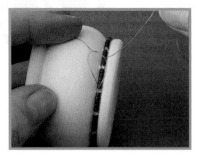

5 Place the beaded thread round the bottom rim of the pot and tie it on with a double knot.

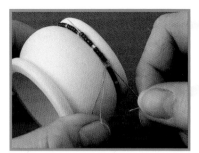

6 Stitch through eleven of the beads: five plum, one gold and five plum.

7 Trim one end of the thread. Thread the needle with the other end of the thread and repeat steps 6 and 7.

8 Repeat steps 1 to 6 to make a beaded ring for the top rim of the pot. Trim the short end of the thread, without the needle. Then take the needle through five plum beads and one gold bead.

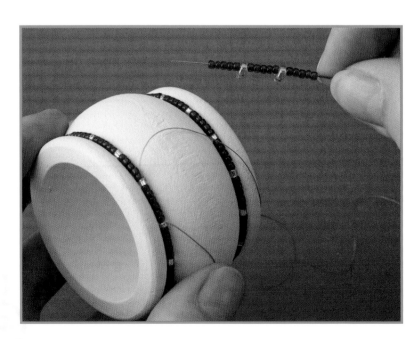

9 Pick up five plum beads, a magatama, five plum, a magatama and five plum.

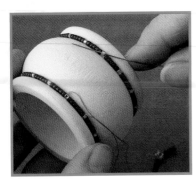  

|O Stitch through a gold bead on the bottom row.

| | Pull the thread through and pick up five plum, a magatama and five plum beads.

|2 Go up through the top magatama on the vertical row of beads.

|3 Pick up five plum beads and stitch through the next gold bead on the top edge.

|4 Pick up five plum beads, one magatama and five plum beads, and stitch down through the bottom magatama on the vertical row of beads.

|5 Pick up five plum beads and go through the next gold bead on the bottom row.

16 Continue stitching round, repeating the pattern, until there is just one gold bead left unstitched on the bottom rim.

17 Pick up five plum beads and stitch into the last gold bead on the bottom rim.

18 Pick up five plum beads and go up through the bottom magatama in the first vertical row.

19 Pick up five plum beads and go up through the magatama from the end of the bead netting.

20 Pick up five plum beads and stitch up into the gold bead on the top edge, where you started.

21 Stitch through six beads along the top edge.

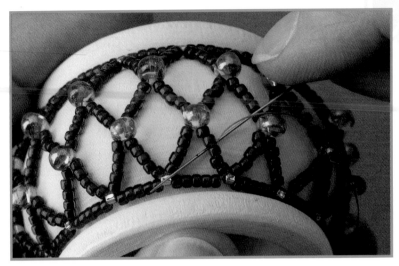

22 Take the needle through three beads on a diagonal row.

23 Take the needle under the row as shown.

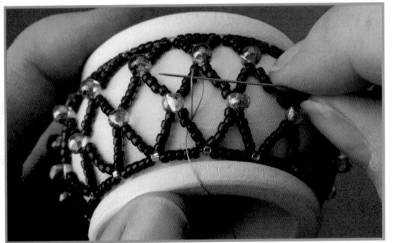

24 Make a loop and stitch through it to knot the thread.

25 Stitch through 2cm (¾in) of beads to hide the thread.

26 Trim the end. Rethread the needle with the tail of thread you left at the start and repeat steps 21 to 26.

Keep your special treasures in this beautiful Trinket Pot.

What next?

Paint the pot to go with
your bedroom and
choose beads that
look good with
the paint.

Bugle Necklace

Once you have mastered making a single stranded necklace like the Ethnic Pendant, you can move on to this triple strand design. Pinks, purples and clear glass make this a really bright and vibrant necklace that you will love to wear.

You will need

Size 10 beading needle

2m (80in) lilac Nymo B beading thread

135 (or 2g) size 11 pink seed beads

Eighty-six (or 4g) purple 6mm bugle beads

Forty-two 4mm (⅛in) round glass beads

Fifteen 6mm (¼in) round glass beads

Magnetic clasp

Sharp scissors

The pattern for the Bugle Necklace.

TOP TIP!

Some bugle beads have sharp or cracked edges which might cut your thread. Discard these and only use perfect bugles.

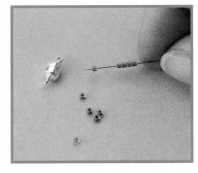

1 Thread a size 10 beading needle with the lilac beading thread. Pick up five size 11 pink seed beads.

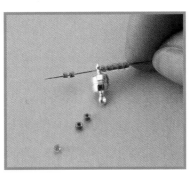

2 Pick up the magnetic clasp and then five more pink seed beads.

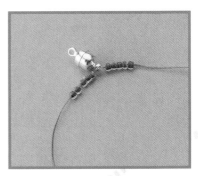

3 Push the beads and clasp down the thread, leaving a 15cm (6in) tail.

4 Make a loop with the thread, left over right, and put the needle through it to make a knot as shown.

5 Make a second knot, right over left.

6 Pull the knot tight to make a little ring of pink beads. Then use your needle to pick up a pink seed bead, a bugle bead, a pink seed bead, a purple 6mm round glass bead, a pink seed bead, a purple bugle, a pink seed bead and a 4mm round glass bead.

7 Repeat until you have threaded fifteen of the 6mm round glass beads, then pick up a pink seed bead, a bugle and another pink seed bead.

8 Pick up five pink seed beads and put the needle through the free end of the clasp.

9 Pick up another five pink seed beads. Pull the thread through and stitch through the five seed beads from step 8, the end of the clasp, and the last five seed beads.

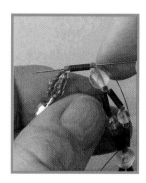

10 Now stitch back through a pink seed bead, a bugle bead, a pink seed bead, a 6mm round glass bead and a pink seed bead as shown.

11 Pick up a bugle, a pink, a 4mm round glass bead, a pink and a bugle. Now stitch back along the necklace, going through a pink, a 6mm round glass bead and another pink.

12 Continue all the way back along the necklace in this way, until you come out of the last 6mm bead and stitch through a pink, a bugle and a pink.

 **13** Stitch through the five pink beads at the end.

 **14** Now stitch through the end of the clasp and the other five pink beads.

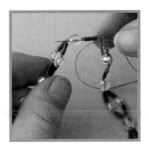 **15** Go back through a pink, a bugle, a pink, a 6mm round glass bead and a pink.

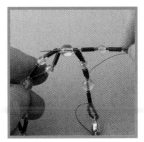 **16** Pick up a bugle, a pink, a 4mm round glass bead, a pink and a bugle and go through a pink, a 6mm round glass bead and a pink.

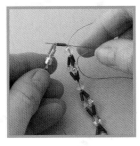 **17** Continue to the last 6mm round glass bead and go through a pink, a bugle and a pink.

 **18** Go through the five seed beads at the end again.

 **19** Stitch through the end of the clasp and through the other five seed beads that side of the clasp.

 **20** Stitch through a pink, a bugle and a pink.

 **21** Make a loop by passing the needle under the thread.

 **22** Stitch through the loop to make a knot.

 **23** You have now secured the end of the necklace but you need to hide the end of the thread. Do this by stitching through 3cm (1¼in) of beads.

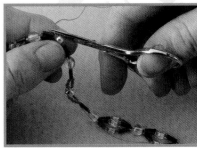 **24** Snip off the end of the thread using sharp scissors. Repeat steps 21 to 24 to finish off the tail of thread you left at the beginning of the necklace.

This simple yet classic Bugle Necklace will be the envy of all your friends.

TOP TIP!

When you are hiding the end of the thread, pull it tight and cut it close to the beads. It will shrink back inside the beads.

What next?

Try other colour combinations like red, gold and black or choose metallic and pearl beads to match your mood or your outfit!

Mini Bag

This exquisite little bag is made using a beading technique called <u>peyote stitch</u> with blue cube beads, and it is decorated with shimmering seed beads and a beaded fringe. It will take some time to make, but is well worth the effort.

You will need

Size 10 beading needle

40g blue 4mm cubes

30g size 11 blue seed beads

Two size 11 white seed beads

Nymo D beading thread

Scissors

TOP TIP!

Whenever your thread starts to look short, look at the box on page 38, which shows you how to finish it off and join in a new one.

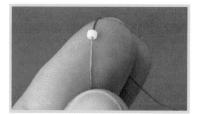

1 Thread a beading needle with a 150cm (59in) length of beading thread. Thread on a white bead 15cm (6in) from the end.

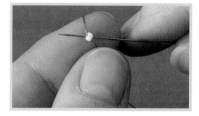

2 Stitch through the white bead again to tie it on. This is a 'stop bead'. It is there to prevent the other beads from sliding off the thread. It will be removed later.

3 Use the needle to pick up fifteen blue cube beads.

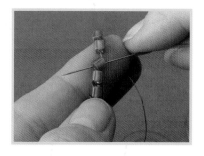

4 Miss out the two cube beads nearest the needle and stitch back through the third cube.

5 Pull the thread tight as shown.

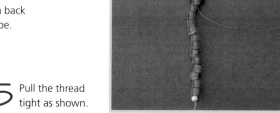

6 Pick up one cube, miss a cube on the first row and stitch into the next bead.

7 Continue down the row, picking up a bead, missing one bead on the base row and stitching into the next. This is called peyote stitch.

8 Pick up a cube and stitch into one of the raised cubes.

9 Continue to the end of the row as shown.

10 Keep going until you have twenty-eight cube beads across the top and bottom as shown. This is the main body of the bag.

11 You need to 'zip' the bag together now. Pull the sides together. Stitch through a raised bead from the other side.

12 Stitch through a raised bead from the bottom side.

TOP TIP!
You need to pull the stitches quite tight.

13 Continue along the side of the bag, 'zipping' it in the same way.

14 When you reach the end, pull off the 'stop' bead.

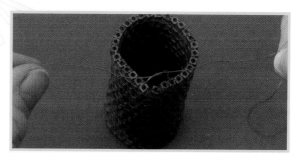

15 Pull the thread tight, then knot the ends of the thread twice.

37

16 Flatten the bag. The join should be down the middle of the back. You have now made the main body of the bag.

17 Now you need to get round to the front of the bag to begin decorating it. At the back, stitch down through one cube.

18 Then stitch up through the next cube.

19 Continue stitching in this way round to the front of the bag. You are ready to start decorating the bag with blue seed beads.

Finishing off and joining in threads

When you are about to run out of thread, use these steps to finish off your old thread so that the end will not show. Use A and B to join in a new thread.

A Go down through a cube at the edge of the bag.

B Go down through the next cube.

C Snip the end of the thread.

20 Pick up three size 11 seed beads. Miss one cube and stitch down into the next one.

21 Pick up three more seed beads, miss a cube and stitch down into the next one.

22 At the end of the row, stitch through the bead on the far right.

23 Stitch in the other direction through the next cube along.

24 Repeat steps 20 to 21 up the next row of cubes. At the end of that row, turn again by repeating steps 22 and 23. Continue beading up and down the rows until the front of the bag is beaded as shown.

25 Now you need to join the bottom of the bag. Stitch from back to front, going under the two threads that join the cubes.

26 Continue in this way across the bottom of the bag.

27 At the end, stitch down through one cube.

28 Take the thread round to the back of the back and stitch up through the next cube.

29 To begin the fringe, pick up forty seed beads and stitch through the cube at the front of the bag.

30 Stitch down through the next cube at the front.

31 Pick up forty-five beads and stitch through the cube at the back of the bag.

32 Repeat steps 29 to 31, picking up five more beads each time, until you reach 70 beads in the middle of the bag.

33 Continue across the bag, decreasing the number of beads by five each time, until you finish with forty at the other end.

34 Stitch in and out of cubes in order to get the needle and thread from the bottom corner of the bag to the top left.

35 Now begin the top trim. Pick up seven seed beads. Miss one cube and stitch down through the next one, working left to right.

36 Stitch back up through the cube you missed before, to the left.

37 Pick up another seven seed beads. Miss one cube and go down into the next one on the right.

38 Work across the front of the bag.

39 Work across the back of the bag in the same way.

TOP TIP!
You will probably need to finish off your thread and start a new one to begin the strap.

40 To begin the strap, bring the needle up through the cube bead at the top left-hand corner.

41 Pick up twenty seed beads and one cube.

42 Repeat step 41 thirty times, ending with twenty seed beads. Stitch down into the top right-hand cube at the back of the bag.

43 Come up through the cube at the top right-hand side of the bag front.

44 Pick up twenty seed beads and go through the first cube in the bag's strap.

45 Pick up twenty more seed beads and stitch through the next cube in the strap.

46 Continue until you come back to the start of the strap, and stitch down into the top left-hand cube at the back of the bag. Finish off your thread in the usual way.

Your beautiful Mini Bag will look great swinging against your hip.

What next?

Try different colour combinations. Purple and silver beads look amazing. Once you have got the hang of it, you can make a larger bag for your phone or small change.

Friendship Bracelet

Friendship bracelets are traditionally made to give to a friend. Some people believe that you should never take the bracelet off, but wear it until it falls off naturally, otherwise the friendship will end!
Beadweaving was developed by the Native Americans. The warp threads are the long threads that run the length of the loom. The weft threads are the ones in the needle that you weave in and out of the warp threads.

You will need

Nymo B beading thread

Indian bead loom

Size 10 beading needle

Sixty-seven (or 2g) purple size 11 seed beads

333 (or 5g) lilac size 11 seed beads

246 (or 4g) white size 11 seed beads

168 (or 3g) pink size 11 seed beads

Scissors

One 8mm fire-polished bead

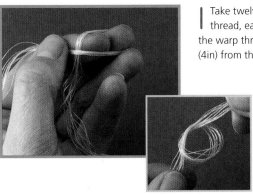

I Take twelve strands of beading thread, each 70cm (27½in) long, for the warp threads. Make a loop 10cm (4in) from the end and tie a knot.

Finish here

The pattern for the Friendship Bracelet.

TOP TIP!

Follow the chart from bottom left to top right.

2 Split the threads into two lots of six.

Start here

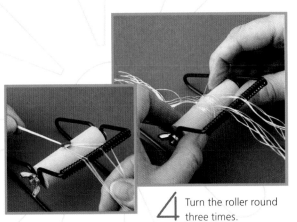

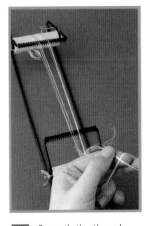

4 Turn the roller round three times.

3 Place the knot behind the nail at the far end of the bead loom, with six threads on either side.

5 Smooth the threads and tie a knot at the other end of the threads.

6 Lift up the slack threads with your right hand and fix the new knot round the front roller.

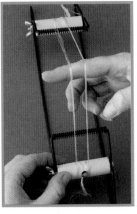

7 Turn the front roller towards you to wind up the excess thread.

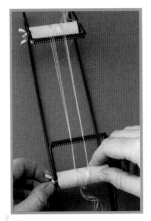

8 Tighten the front roller and turn the wing nut to secure it.

9 Arrange the threads between the notches of the springs as shown.

The twelve threads should now look like this.

10 Thread the needle with 150cm (59in) of thread. This will be the weft thread.

11 Tie it on to the left-hand warp thread about 2cm (¾in) from the springs in the loom, leaving a 15cm (6in) tail.

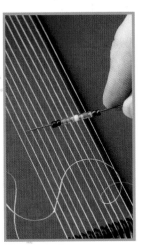

12 Use the needle to pick up the first row of beads: two purple, three lilac, one white, three lilac and two purple. The pattern on page 42 shows all the rows of beads.

43

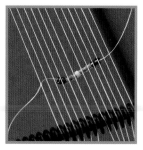 13 Take the needle and thread under the warp threads.

 14 Push up the row of beads so that there is one bead between each thread.

 15 Put the needle back through the threads, right to left, on top of the warp threads.

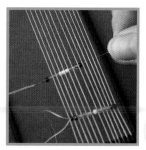 16 Pick up one purple bead, three lilac, three white, three lilac and one purple.

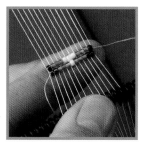 17 Pull the needle through from left to right, then pass the thread under the warp threads and push them up as before.

 18 Put the needle back through the row of beads from right to left on top of the warp threads.

 19 Continue in the same way, following the pattern on page 42. You will start to see the pattern as shown.

 20 When there is only about 15cm (6in) of weft thread left, go back one row and stitch through the beads from left to right.

TOP TiP!

Your thread will not be long enough to finish the whole bracelet, so you need to finish your thread and start a new one. Steps 20 to 25 show how to finish your old thread and start a new one so that the ends will not show.

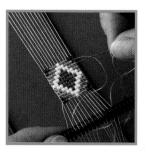 21 Go back another row and stitch from right to left.

 22 Repeat two more times and trim the end of the thread very close to the beads. The end will now be hidden.

 23 Thread the needle with another 150cm (59in) length of thread. Go back three rows and stitch from right to left.

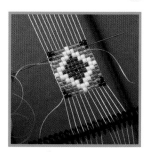 24 Leave a 5cm (2in) tail and stitch through the second row from left to right.

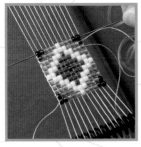  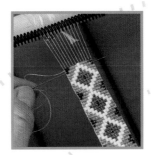 

25 Stitch through the top row. Now you are ready to continue with the pattern.

26 Wind the beaded section down as you work.

27 At the end of the bracelet, you need to weave the end of the thread back through the work to hide it. Come back one row and stitch through it from left to right.

28 Stitch through the third row back from right to left.

  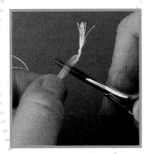 

29 Continue to the fifth row back and trim the end of the thread.

30 Loosen the wing nut on the front roller, wind it back and take the bracelet off the loom.

31 Trim the knots off the ends of the bracelet.

32 Thread the needle with the right-hand warp thread and stitch under the thread at the side of the bracelet.

33 Repeat the stitch four times down the side.

34 Stitch through all the beads in the sixth row.

35 Thread the needle with the second warp thread and catch a warp thread one row back as shown.

36 Continue back to the fifth row, catching the thread in the same way as shown. Then stitch through the sixth row of beads.

37 Repeat for the third, fourth and fifth warp threads. With some, stitch back six rows and stitch through the seventh. This will stop the sixth row of beads from getting blocked. Repeat steps 32 to 33 with the twelfth thread, stitching up the other side of the bracelet. Then repeat steps 34 and 35 with the seventh, eighth, ninth, tenth and eleventh warp threads.

38 Secure all the warp threads apart from the middle one in this way. When securing the last one, stitch back six rows and stitch through the seventh row as shown.

39 Pull all the threads tight and trim them. Trim both sides of the bracelet.

40 Thread the needle with the last thread in the middle. Pick up five lilac beads, one 8mm fire-polished bead and three lilac beads.

41 Stitch back through the 8mm fire-polished bead and the five lilac beads.

42 Stitch through the white bead and the rest of the row right to left, as shown.

43 Stitch through the second row, left to right.

44 Stitch through the third row, right to left.

45 Stitch through the fourth row, left to right, then through the fifth row, right to left. Trim the thread.

46 Repeat steps 31 to 44 to finish the other end of the bracelet, leaving the thread in the middle. Thread the needle with it and pick up five lilac beads and one pink bead.

47 Pick up 18–20 lilac beads and go back through the pink bead, towards the bracelet.

48 Pull the thread through to make a loop, and check that this fits over the bobble bead at the other end of the bracelet.

49 Put the needle through the five lilac beads towards the bracelet.

50 Stitch back through the white bead on the first row and through to the end of the row, right to left.

51 Stitch through the second, third, fourth and fifth rows, changing direction with each row. Trim the end of the thread.

What next?

Beading on a loom is great for making long, straight-sided pieces. Why not try a choker, a hat band or even a beaded belt?

Make friendship bracelets for all your friends! Boys might like earthy colours and ethnic looking designs.

More books to read

The Bead Jewellery Maker by Cheryl Owen, Collins & Brown, 2005
Beginner's Guide to Beadwork by Madeleine Rollason, Search Press, 2004
Daisy Chains – A Beginner's Guide to Using Seed Beads by Heather Kingsley-Heath, The Useful Booklet Company, 2002
The Encyclopedia of Beading Techniques by Sara Withers & Stephanie Burnham, Search Press, 2005

Useful websites

http://www.gjbeads.co.uk/
http://www.beadworkersguild.org.uk/
http://beadwork.about.com/

http://www.craftbits.com
(Click on Bead Crafts on the left-hand menu)
http://members.tripod.com/kyal/patterns/links.html

Glossary

Beadweaving Weaving beads together by hand or by using a loom.
Bohemian From the former kingdom of Bohemia, in the modern day Czech Republic.
Ceramic A hard, brittle material made by firing clay or other substances in a kiln.
Faceted bead A bead made to look like a crystal or a cut gemstone, with many small, flat, polished surfaces.
Fire-polished bead Another name for a faceted bead.
Native Americans The original people from North America, also known as American Indians.
Peyote stitch A beadweaving technique used by Native Americans. It is done by hand, without a loom.
Sinew The cord or band of tissue that attaches a muscle to a bone.
Zulu People of southeast Africa, living mainly in northeast Natal province in South Africa.

Index